She always loved the stars

Poppy Grey

Presentation by *BookLeaf Publishing*

Web: www.bookleafpub.com

E-mail: info@bookleafpub.com

ISBN: 9789357445078

First edition 2021

PREFACE

TRIGGER WARNING: This book contains strong themes and references to depression, self harm, disordered eating and suicide please DO NOT READ if you know this will effect you in anyway and seek help!

Samaritans: 116 123
Text SHOUT to 85258
Or even the website https://www.7cups.com helped me a lot

The Beginning

It makes sense to start here,
Right at the beginning.

This story has no order,
You're just meant to dip in and out
Like I do of happiness.
Because what follows is the jumbled mess
Of thoughts in my mind that I cannot speak out
loud,
But I long to express,
And share with the world.

But I've lost my train of thought,
This was meant to be a story,
Of how we ended up here;
These words, their worry (or lack of).

She grew up happy, careless and free,
But something changed when she turned
thirteen.
Her compassion, and kindness, and selflessness
grew,
But deep in her mind the joy had bloomed, into
something darker;
Scary and strong,

Something infected her and it didn't take long
For the smiles on her face to be faker than a
Barbie,
And those closest to her no longer knew her
story.

And seven years later, she's been through hell,
She isn't out of it yet, but she does now know,
How to cope as best she can with the emotions
she's given,
And write stories of heartbreak so she doesn't
give in,
To the dangerous addiction of blade and blood,
And the words in her head don't drown her for
good.

She always loved the Stars

She was 3 years old, maybe 4,
And she loved watching the stars.
Loved lying on the sand counting them,
Or drawing patterns with her little hand;
But her sweet small mind was so sad to learn
that
Something so beautiful,
Could be so far away.

She was 9 years old, maybe 10,
And she loved learning about the stars
She was sat in science taking it all in,
Realising at their core, they were just massive
balls of gas and flame,
And her still childish mind was curious,
As to how something so beautiful,
Could be so capable of destruction.

She was 13 years old, maybe 14,
And for some reason she still loved the stars.
When her troubled heart filled her life with
darkness,

And Pinterest filled her eyes with cringe worthy
quotes
Of stars as their everlasting symbol of hope;
But she knew that wasn't true, and they ended
their life as a black hole.
But still her dark and twisted mind saw beauty in
the stars,
Even if she didn't see hope.

She was 16 years old, maybe 17,
And she still loved the stars.
She'd search them for hope,
To help her through the night;
And even though most nights it's cloudy,
And she doesn't see them often,
She still loves the stars
And believes soon she'll be among them.

She is 19 years old, maybe 20,
And she loves watching the stars.
She took her boyfriend to the sand and they lay
there
Hand in hand,
And she'd look at the stars and smile,
because they were so beautiful and so constant,
And even if they were covered by clouds
Or drowned in the city lights,
They were still there watching over her,
Just like when she was little.

I don't know grief, but I do know sadness

I don't know grief, but I do know sadness

I don't know how it feels to lose someone
you've known all your life,
Someone who has been by your side through
thick and thin,
Someone who knows all your stories,
Not because you told them, but because they
lived them too.

I don't know how it feels to have a good day and
want nothing more than to go home and tell your
favourite person,
But they aren't there,
And they'll never know.

I don't know how it feels to wake up in the
morning and reach for someone
Whose side of the bed is now cold forever,
And will never see the sunrise again,

And will never meet their grandchildren
And will never get to walk their daughter down
the aisle,
Or retire and travel thousands of miles.

But I do know how it feels to wake up in the
morning,
And not know how you're going to face the day.
I know how it feels when they look at you with
pity in their eyes and all that makes you feel is
anger.
Anger at them for thinking they know how you
feel, for sympathizing with your sorrow; how
could they truly know the vast emptiness in the
pit of your stomach, and the constant ache of
your heart with every beat it takes and the way
your breath shakes trying to force out
meaningless words and the sting of tears that
always lingers behind your eyes.

And then guilt for wishing they knew how you
felt because, in reality, you'd never wish this
pain on anyone else, especially those trying their
best for you.

I don't know grief, but I do know sorrow.
And although its not the same,
Tell me what you need,
Because I know you're not okay.

Alone

The fact that no one knew,
Fucking hurt.

When she told him,
One of her closest friends,
One of the few people she wanted to tell
everything to,
One of the people she trusted the most in this
world,
He was shocked, and she didn't know why.

Surely he knew her well enough to know
She was too broken to cry,
That when she laughed at her co worker's jokes
It was all a ruse; she smiled to lie.

She wanted him to know,
So she had someone to talk to,
But how he reacted, she doubted he'd know
what to do
Or say when she told him how she felt,
Or if she needed encouragement not to kill
herself.

She wanted him there,

To be on her side,
She likes being alone so she doesn't have to hide
Who she really is and how broken she feels,

But his basic boy brain,
Found it too much to handle.

Scars and Stretch marks

Her skin is ripping at its seams,
The little girl doesn't know what it means,
When rivers of pink scars create a map on her
thighs,
She runs and asks
"Mum, what are these lines?"

She hates the way they've tarnished
Her smooth unbroken skin,
A sign that she was growing,
And no longer fitting in.

Her mother smiled down at her and said,
"Honey don't worry, it's just a part of life,
The scars they'll stay with you, but don't you
worry,
They'll fade in time".

But as they faded, new scars took their place,
Ones formed not of growth but burnt in out of
hate.

The girl was no longer innocent, her smile no
longer bright,
Some days she even doubted she'd make it
through the night.

And when her mother saw these scars, she
frowned so she wouldn't cry,
Begging her daughter,
"Please, just tell me why?
These scars may fade but they will be with you
for life."

The daughter was confused, she couldn't
understand
The difference between what nature caused and
what she did by her own hand. Those white
marks that ran across her body,
Mapping rivers and ravines,
Were the stories of her life, what she'd done and
where she'd been.

And although she mostly hides them
In a shroud of guilt and shame,
Alone in her apartment, to her, they look the
same.

They were signs of growth and healing
And they made her who she was.

The Artist

They see her bored doodles
Scribbled in the margins,
But she has always hidden her masterpieces,
Canvases of soft and pale skin,
With bases of pinks and white,
Flashes of silver
Paint crimson.
So much crimson,
Blooming like a rose,
Drowning the pale snow beneath.

They hear her songs of sorrow and loss,
But not the words they speak.
They don't see through her morbid jokes,
The desperate plea,
The cry for help, You're gonna lose me.

Days like this, Days like that

Some days, the scars don't seem so bright,
The marks on her thighs blend in to the night.
The glare of the stars shines light in her eyes,
And the tears she cries help her feel alive.

But there are days in darkness, More common
than not,
Where her scars scream out "We're all so alone!"
Pick up the knife, drag it across your skin,
Look at that red,
God, you wished it would sting"

And tears she can't cry,
For some reason her eyes have never felt so dry,
And when they see her she smiles,
For they can't see the trials
She runs in her brain, ruining her mind,
Her relationships.
But it's alright,
She's just fine.

Cold

Lying alone
Naked on the bathroom floor,
Staring at the ceiling,
Alone with you fears,
No thoughts,
And only the cold grip of darkness
To keep you warm.

Chefs are just socially acceptable masochists

It was her first day of a new job,
But despite all the normal anxieties, her biggest
fear was the uniform:
Short Sleeved, Black T-shirt.

But then when she got there,
And they took her into the changing room,
They revealed they were just like her.
With arms of scars, burns, cuts and bruises
And charcoal circles under their eyes
And cracked forced half smiles.

And after half a day there, surrounded by every
trigger,
She realised they were just like her,
Obsessed with knives and fire.
And working until their feet bled,
And focusing in so much depth, on everything
but their own thoughts.

They were just like her,
But maybe they didn't notice,
The destruction of their body
For a little piece of mind.
"That's just chef life" they'd say,
And despite being new, she knew,

Chefs are just socially acceptable masochists,
And that's what she was too.

Recovery

When you're happy, you wish never to be sad
again.
When you're sad, you don't believe you will
ever be happy again.
But how can you miss the sun without the
clouds?
And how can you love the stars without the clear
dark night?

She is out the other side, almost,
But she will never be the same.
She hides her delicate arms
With white scars that scratch the surface of the
red hidden in her mind.

She couldn't hide them in the kitchen where she
worked,
But they didn't ask so she didn't tell.
She kept them hidden from the rest of the
world,
For all they knew, she was perfectly well.

They are the fear of knives she struggles with as
a chef,
Learning to cut again without bleeding.

They are the paper cuts that sting in the shower,
Reminding her of what else used to sting.
They are grabbing the back wall of the
platform,
'cos she always feared she might jump.
They are the shallow baths from fear of
drowning.
Almost.

Almost.

Intimate with Darkness

You were never the pretty girl,
Always too chubby and awkward,
Too tall and clumsy.

And as you grew into a teenager,
And high school standings were everything,
You sank alone into a dark corner of the room.

And as your friends went off, drinking cider in
the park,
And kissing boys they claimed they hated
You became closer with darkness and further
from their nature.

Darkness taught you a different kind of intimacy,
One that didn't rely on anybody,
You caused all your own heartbreak,
Drew all your own scars,
Talked you onto the ledge,
But never pushed you too far.

Darkness teaches you to survive just fine on
your own,
'Cos how much damage can their shallow words
do,
If your own thoughts chill you to the bone?
And how much can their punches hurt,
If you slice your own skin just to feel home?

It's a dangerous dance becoming intimate with
darkness,
Because as warm and as safe as it feels,
You have to kill that part of yourself
If you ever want the light back in.

Losing innocence

She dreamt kisses by the campfire
And dancing in the rain,
Of light summer dresses
And posh balls, with champagne.

She lived her life with her heart in the clouds
Where fantasy and romance
Made her laugh more than frown.

But as she grew up she shifted her mind
And although her soul was hard,
Her heart still pined
For fairy tales of love, and dancing, and princes.

Her mind was now a dark room, with lights of
red,
Where her thoughts now wandered to war, and
sex, and death,
And the blood from her heart that dripped on the
floor,
Stained her stories of love, and made her look
like a whore.

Those campfire kisses now tasted of smoke,
And dancing in the rain was only ever fuelled by
coke.
Supermarket vodka filled the glasses at the ball
And her short skin tight dress would be the
reason he'd call.

It wasn't the love she needed but it was still love

She's been alone all her life,
Her trust thinner than her scarred fragile skin,
And her walls are built higher than the stars she gazes at.

So she searches for validation in drunken strangers,
And accepts their sloppy kisses,
And doesn't give a shit what her so called 'friends' think.
'Cos if she can't feel loved in sober reality,
A drunken dream will have to do.

He could be Anyone

He could be anyone
You didn't get attatched to him,
You got attatched to a feeling.
The way you felt lying beside him with your
hands on his chest and his fingers through your
hair,
His warm hug after the cold night air,
The kiss on your forehead to silently tell you he
cared.
The world is a dangerous place, but that didn't
matter,
Not when his sea blue eyes washed away your
pain.
The world is a lonely place, but that didn't
matter,
Not when you felt so safe in his arms.
You keep reminding yourself that he could be
anyone,
He was just the first to show the slightest bit of
interest
After you'd been on your own for so long.
It's not about him,
He could be anyone.

The Traveller and the Pilot

She wanted to see the world,
He wanted to show her.

He'd lead, She'd follow;
He'd fly, She'd fall,
And somehow they would land together.

But two people with their heads in the clouds,
Can so easily lose sight of the ground,
And like the birds he flys with,
He'll migrate South for the winter,
But like the wolves of the North,
She'll always feel at home in the cold.

So He lead and She followed;
He flew and She fell,
And they somehow crashed and broke alone.

Favourite Faded Fantasy- Damien Rice

I didn't fall in love with you,
I fell in love with a fantasy
And used your face to make it a reality.

But even though he looked like you,
And talked like you,
And smelt like you,
The stories are all me.

And in reality,
You aren't who I created you to be.

I thought I wanted love,
What I wanted was someone to choose
Me.
To be a first choice,
Instead of number three.

But even though it was in my mind,

and I knew it was just me,
Maybe some part of me wanted you to be my
reality,

But instead I'm lying here listening to 'My
favourite faded fantasy'.
Cus' that's what you are,
You're My favourite, faded, fantasy.

Nyx

He brought out a darkness in her,
A side she rarely shows.
Maybe, she thought his confidence,
Brought out the same in her,
Although she knew it was all a game,
She was just another girl,
But although she couldn't say it,
She wanted him to know,
That she was who she was,
A queen of darkness,
A goddess of hell.
She wanted him to know that if he messed with her,
This is what he'd get.
'Cus as much as she could love
And as far as she could fall,
Her heart was closely guarded, and if he lost her,
He'd lose it all.

For Real?

They'd spend each Saturday on the sofa,
Drinking beer with their hopes up,
Laughing and kissing and just enjoying the
moment.

And it was all fun and games,
Until her darkness came to haunt her,
And she'd look up at his face and he would be
real no longer.

His sea blue eyes and sandy hair,
Were no longer his features,
To her touch they felt like air.

She'd stop smiling as she looked up at him,
And trace her hand across his skin,
And whisper in his ear, "I never can tell if you're
really here."

And he'd laugh and call her silly,
And say "Of course I'm real, you're literally
holding me,"
And she'd just smile and say "Okay."

But even as she held him there,

She knew her mind and it's thirst for fear,
And she knew to never truly trust the power

Of what a broken mind can tell a broken heart,
That it was too good to be true,
That he was not real, she just wanted someone to
hold on to.

But then the next morning she'd wake up to his
face,
And realise the stupidity of questioning his
embrace,
Because even after her phases of misery and
mistakes,

He was still there, for real, as always.

Fear

She couldn't see,
Her breath the same rhythm as her shaking
scarred hands.
He looked terrified, she wished he'd just look
away.

He'd told her that he loved her,
And she knew it was true,
But what really scared her,
Is she didn't think she could love too.

She knew she cared for him, and wanted him
close,
He was her best friend; he knew her better than
most.
She wanted to say it, so that he'd know,
She cared for him more than her words would
show.

It wasn't his words that scared her,
Really she scared herself.
She didn't think she could love him,
She was too broken to know
What love really felt like,
Or how it would grow.

She had gotten so used to going through life
alone,
Sharing it with someone was a hard skill to
learn.

For once she wasn't scared he'd leave her when
he's bored,
She didn't even worry if he talked to other girls
or forgot to call.
But she was scared of her own darkness,
That it was too much for him to handle.
She was scared that he would bare his soul to
her and
She would leave him stranded.

She wished she could tell him this,
Warn him of her demons,
Instead she just froze in fear and said:
"You can't love me really."
She could see the pain that she had caused,
turning his clear eyes cloudy,
She wanted so much to hold him close and say,
"Give me time and don't give up, and soon
I'll let you love me.

Sunshine boy

She always felt at home in the darkness,
Clinging to the shadows.
Her spirit only drawn
To places she could hide her soul.

Her face matched the sky
On a clear dark night,
Her freckles, the stars,
The only glint of light.

She met a boy,
He wasn't her type,
No tortured soul,
His sunshine seemed too bright.

His hair held sunbeams,
That danced in his seascape eyes,
And his hands held enough warmth
To melt her heart of ice.

He saw this girl of darkness,
And was not afraid,
To go with her everywhere,
Even when she wasn't safe.

Her tortured soul,
She'd believed had been damned,
He held in his arms
And brought slowly back to life.

He did not rush her,
Didn't grab her when she pulled back,
Only waited in the sunlight,
Holding out a welcome hand.

Hades and Persephone

They stood there, back in the place they met
And the sky was a soft baby blue,
That reflected the equally tranquil sea and his
deep bright eyes.

He was smiling at her, and she felt he could see
right through her brown eyes, Right to the
darkest depths of her soul.
And he didn't flinch at what he saw there.
Instead, he saw the clouds and the rain and the
mud and he planted seeds.
And the more it rained in her soul,
The more the seeds grew and flourished into a
garden of beautiful spring flowers.

And gradually the rain slowed and the sun shone
more,
So that even in times of darkness,
She now had something constant to give her
hope.
And proof that she was capable of growth.

He had given that to her.
And in return she had taught him how to accept
and nurture his darkness,
Allowing him to grieve and breathe without it
taking over
And killing the beauty
And life he brought to the world.

Together they were the perfect balance.